D0998046

PAW-SOME
COLOURING

PaRragon

Bath · New York · Cologne · Melbourne · Delhi
Hong Kong · Shenzhen · Singapore · Amsterdam

Here to protect the citizens of Adventure Bay – PAW Patrol!

Ryder is PAW Patrol's commander.

Marshall is a Dalmatian puppy.

He is PAW Patrol's fireman!

Chase is a German Shepherd.

He is PAW Patrol's police pup!

Rocky is a mixed-breed puppy.

He is PAW Patrol's recycling dog!

Rubble is a Bulldog.

He is PAW Patrol's building expert!

Skye is a cute Cockapoo puppy.

She's a real adventurer!

Zuma is a Labrador pup.

He is PAW Patrol's water-rescue dog.

Ryder runs to the Lookout – PAW Patrol's headquarters.

When he needs to summon the PAW Patrol,
Ryder contacts them with his PupPad.

Zuma and Skye's dog tags light up
when Ryder calls them to the Lookout.

Rocky and Rubble run to the Lookout.

Chase and Marshall run to the Lookout, too.

"**Whenever there's trouble, just yelp for help!**"

Ryder drives an all-terrain vehicle.
It can turn into a jet-ski or even a snowmobile.

He rides it on lots of PAW Patrol missions.

When there's an emergency, Chase's Pup House
can turn into a police van.

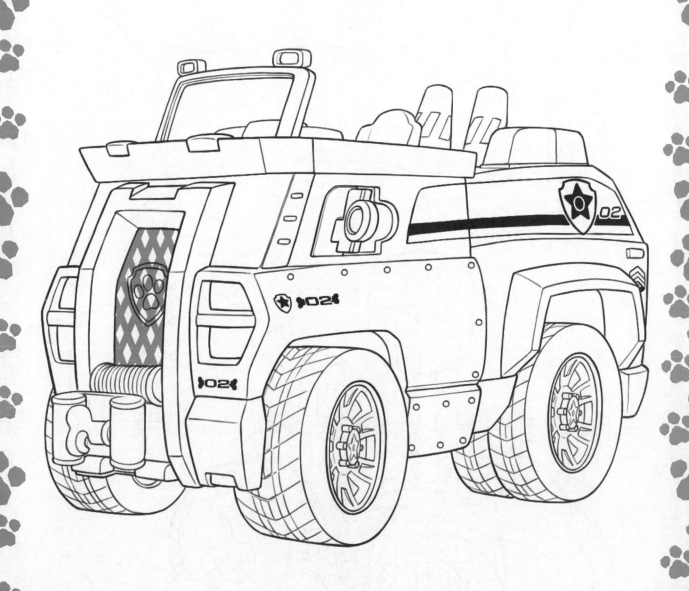

"These paws uphold the laws,"
says Chase as he drives his van.

**Marshall's Pup House turns into a
fire engine with a tall ladder!**

"Ready for a ruff-ruff-rescue!" shouts Marshall.

**Rocky's Pup House turns into
an amazing recycling lorry.**

"Why trash it when you can stash it?" asks Rocky.

Skye's Pup House becomes a helicopter when she needs to fly to the rescue!

"Pups away!" shouts Skye, as she uses her jet pack to soar through the clouds.

**Zuma's Pup House transforms
into a speedy hovercraft.**

"Ready, set, get wet!" says Zuma
as he zips along in his hovercraft.

**Rubble's Pup House becomes a digger –
complete with a drill!**

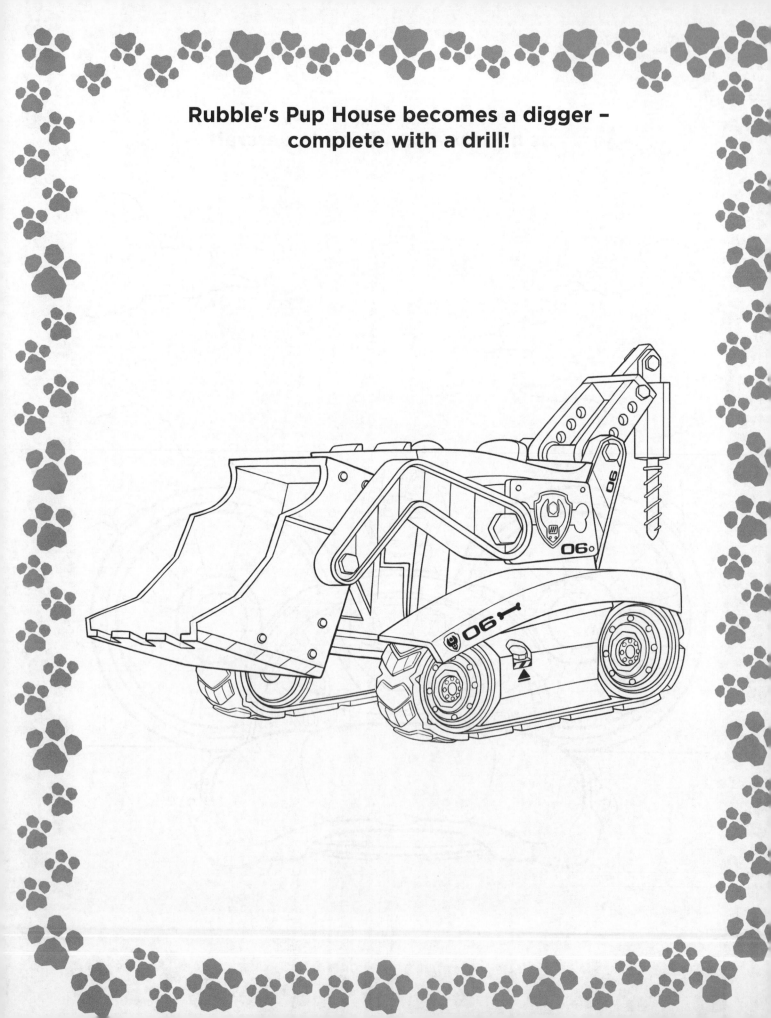

"I can dig it!" says Rubble.

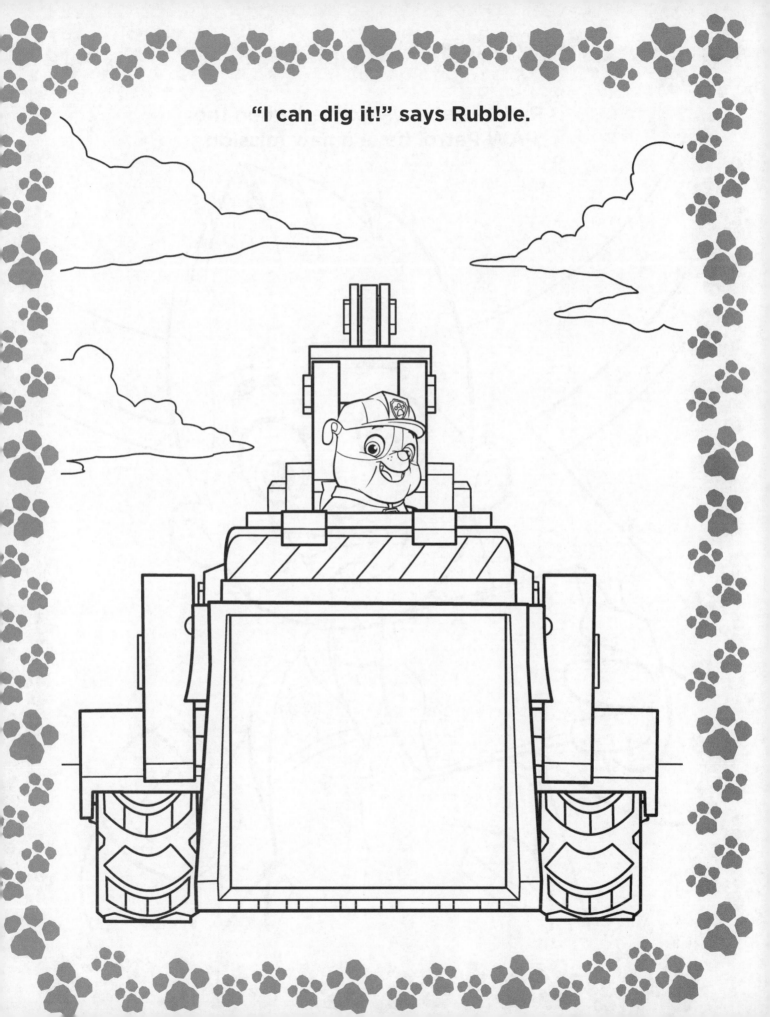

Ryder is always excited when the
PAW Patrol have a new mission.

Ryder tells Chase about a farmer who needs their help.

PAW Patrol have come to help Farmer Yumi take in the harvest.

The tall ladder on Marshall's fire engine is perfect for reaching high branches.

"Chase is on the case!" says Chase,
as he runs to start work.

Skye and Zuma fly in to help, too.

Chase begins by collecting apples.

Rubble can carry so many apples in his digger!

Rubble's digger is very useful at harvest time.

Marshall, Rocky, Rubble and Chase roll some pumpkins to Farmer Yumi's barn.

Marshall gets stuck inside a pumpkin but
Farmer Yumi helps him out!

Ryder and the team are always happy to help out.

**Mayor Goodway is the hard-working
mayor of Adventure Bay.**

Mayor Goodway has a pet chicken called Chickaletta.

Katie lives in Adventure Bay.
She's good friends with the PAW Patrol.

Katie looks after all the pups at her shop – Katie's Pet Parlour.

Katie and Ryder are good friends.

Katie owns a cat called Cali.

Alex is a friend to the PAW Patrol.
He calls on them when he needs help.

"PAW Patrol – here to help!"

PAW Patrol is on the job!

"Let's dive in!" shouts Zuma, as he leaps into the water.

"Rubble on the double!" says the building expert
when he runs to the Lookout.

**"My nose knows!" Chase calls
when he's on the scent.**

"PAW Patrol run to the rescue!"

**Wally the Walrus is stuck on shore.
He needs a helping paw from the pups!**

Ryder leads the way!

**Chase fires a net from his Pup Pack
and helps Wally back in to the sea.**

"No job is too big, no pup is too small!"